The Ten Commandments

For

Business

What I Learned from God In the Workplace

Pray the Lord of the harvest to send out laborers into His harvest. (Matt. 9.38)

Joseph P. Stringer

Vivere Press

ISBN: 978-0-9903301-4-1
ebook ISBN: 978-0-9903301-5-8

Printed in Charleston, South Carolina

Vivere Press

www.josephpstringer.com

Dedication

For my friends at God in the Workplace. Your witness has been an inspiration. May God pour out His blessings on you in life, in business and in this nation.

Acknowledgements:

I first acknowledge Jesus Christ as my Lord and Savior. Without Him, neither this book nor my life would be possible. He has taught me that we should seek to touch the surface of that ocean of love which is His grace.

Second, I most gratefully acknowledge and thank God in the Workplace for the inspiration which they and their speakers have provided for this book. Although the germination of the Ten Commandments For Business was there a decade ago, the ideas needed fertile soil, water and care for them to flourish. GITW has provided these and more. Blessings to this ministry. We will find that its role is a crucial one of witness within our current culture.

Third, I always acknowledge my wife of 42 years, Kathleen. She is my best friend, my sharpest critic, and greatest fan. Kathleen, I love you beyond words.

Fourth, Charleston Southern University, whose leadership in Christian business has been inspirational in bringing Charleston to a new awareness of our Workplace calling.

Finally, I joyfully welcome and acknowledge the South Carolina Christian Chamber of Commerce. It is through this new, growing Christian ministry that we will see revival in this nation.

THE TEN COMMANDMENTS

FOR

BUSINESS

Prologue

Rejoice and be glad, for we are in the midst of battle. We are in tribulation. The secular powers and forces of this age align against Christians, to silence our witness, to oppress our churches and to erase our faith.

For Christians, this age is no different from any other. Jesus himself told his followers, ***"Blessed are you when men revile you and persecute you and utter all kinds of evil against you falsely on my account." (Matt. 5.11)*** In John 16.33 He promises us ***"...in this world you have tribulation."*** Paul teaches us to rejoice in our afflictions. Augustine preached of the City of God and the City of Man: that we are to be in this world, but not of it. Aquinas strove against the unbelievers of his time with the same arguments we make today. Luther shook the foundations of a lukewarm church and returned us to our spiritual roots.

Again, I say rejoice, for we are in good company. We rejoice because Jesus has promised us, ***"...do not fear, for I have overcome the world.***"

This is a war of contrasting beliefs. In America, the weapons our opponents use are social pressure, propaganda, secular law...and commerce.

Yes, commerce is one of their weapons. For too long, business has served the purpose of man rather than the will of God. In America, we surrendered the marketplace to secular forces long ago. It was easy. We were tempted by false promises of a freedom based in man's choices. We businessmen were glad to profit from providing those choices.

Because the spearpoint of business was blunted by secular teachings, the walls of our strongholds were breached. Today, the forces of secularism boldly attack Christian business, the family, and the church. In less than one generation we have moved from battle to bare survival in a culture virulently opposed to any authority besides man's own autonomous choices.

Many secular leaders are consciously seeking to destroy Christ's church. Many others simply do not understand the harm they cause in "doing business as usual."

How do we fight this war in the business environment? Are we called to battle? Does God even belong in business? What does the Bible have to say about work?

Within scripture, we will find that God is intensely focused upon work. Of the parables Jesus told, at least half had to do with work. Often, His statements about the Kingdom of God used work as an example. The epistles of Paul, James and Peter spoke about work in the Kingdom.

The Old Testament is no different. Jeremiah,

Isaiah, Ecclesiastes, the Psalms and Proverbs, Deuteronomy, Leviticus, Exodus and every other book dealt with work. Finally, in Genesis, in the beginning, God is working. He creates Adam to work also. There we find the characteristics of Godly work:

Productivity. ***"The Lord God took the man and put him in the garden of Eden to till it and keep it." (2.15)***

Creativity. "***...and [God] brought them to the man to see what he would call them." (2.18)***

Fruitfulness. ***"Be fruitful and multiply," (1.28a)***

Responsibility. ***"...and fill the earth and subdue it:" (1.28)***

How do we bring these Genesis traits--Productivity, Creativity, Fruitfulness, Responsibility--into our business lives? Christ, the new Adam, brings us back into grace with the Father. But until His return, we must live, work and witness in a fallen world. Is there a guide for us to apply to business?

We find that guide in God's law: the Ten Commandments. Just as the Commandments direct our personal lives, they also provide a means to understand how we are to act in business. As we study the Ten Commandments more closely, we'll find that they are not only right, but are practical, both for our personal lives and for our work.

Throughout this book, we will search out the positive aspect of each Commandment. What does each Commandment imply that we should be doing? We will soon understand that God, through His Ten Commandments, has provided us with His own Risk Management plan for business.

If we follow His Commandments in business as we do in our personal lives, we will avoid the pitfalls of sin and error. Not surprisingly, we also will find that our business prospers and grows.

I belong to a study group, God in the Workplace, which arose from a Christian ministry focused on the need to consciously bring Jesus Christ into the marketplace. This group of Christian men and women meets eight times a year to witness how they have found ways to center Christ in their work.

Being involved in God in the Workplace has been inspiring. We hear testimony of the power of Jesus in changing lives, through growing both the body and spirit within vocation. I believe this movement is God ordained. We are called to stand upon the Word of God at the front lines of a battle we did not choose.

God calls us to this battle. Business has been in retreat for a long time. It is time to prepare ourselves and to stand. As Paul warns us in Ephesians:

"Therefore, take the whole armor of God that you may be able to withstand in the evil day...and take the helmet of salvation, and the sword of the Spirit, which is the word of God." (Eph. 6.13-17)

The beginnings of that word of God lie in His Ten Commandments. Let us find how each one speaks to our mission in the workplace.

One: The Sacred Exists

"I am the Lord your God, who brought you out of the land of Egypt, out of the house of bondage. You shall have no other gods before Me.

We have forgotten. It has been almost 3500 years since the Ten Commandments were written by the Lord Himself upon the tablets given to Moses.

We have forgotten God's Holiness. ***"Put off your shoes from your feet, for the place on which you are standing is Holy Ground." (Exo. 3.5)***

We have forgotten His power and might. ***"...the Lord descended upon [Mount Sinai] like fire; and the smoke of it went up like the smoke of a kiln, and the whole mountain quaked greatly." (Exo. 19.18)***

We have forgotten that He *is* the sacred. To even touch the Ark of the Covenant which held His Commandments meant death. ***"And the anger of the Lord was kindled against Uzzah; and He smote him because he put forth his hand to the ark; and he died there before God." (1 Chr. 13.9)***

We need to remember. The first lesson we learn from God's law is that ***the Sacred exists***...and it is not me. He is wholly apart and above me. God is God.

I am not. My life is not. My business is not.

Wow! I am *not* the master of my fate. I am *not* the captain of my soul. What a relief! If a Sacred God exists, there are standards apart from my own. I answer to Him, (thank God). I am ***responsible*** to Him.

Without God, man makes his own standards. Atheists or Secularists will tell you, "Man is the standard of all value." Yet, which man? When you push an Atheist to define man, when you drill down, probing and asking "What do you think *man should be?",* the essence of the answer to your question will inevitably be, "I want men to be...like me!"

The Christian businessman knows that God is Lord of his entire life, including his business. That there is a sacred God above him to whom he owes *everything.* That knowledge puts all that follows into perspective.

The first Commandment calls for us to know God the Creator. He is the one who brought forth all that is and who breathed life and spirit into man. He is the one we find first working in Genesis. ***"In the beginning, God." (Gen. 1.1)*** His creation, the stars and heavens and all that exists therein, is made--for us. His love and companionship reach down--to us. Jesus, who is the very bridge between the Father's holiness and our sinfulness, and who taught us to call Him Father, reminded us always that the Father is sacred. We are not God. We rely upon His wisdom, grace and inspiration in all the work that we do.

Yet, we are tempted. It's so tempting, especially for the entrepreneur, the creator, the owner. "This is *my* product. *I* created it. *I've* given all these people jobs. *I've* taught them. *My* service or product helps customers, expands markets and creates wealth. *My* business benefits the community and I give more to charity than anyone I know."

Do we hear the focus? "I, I, I." My friend, Dick Davis, is an expert in turning around failing businesses. He has told me that the greatest challenge in any struggling business is: the guy running it. The owner is so focused on self, on his invulnerability, that he creates the very elements which undermine the company's health. Dick calls this "the Superman Syndrome." I'd call it "the God Syndrome." That owner has forgotten that there is a "higher authority" to whom he must answer.

That's the common element in any of our sins. We want to be the one running things! "I'm in charge here!" It's no less damaging when we seek to be in charge in our business, even if our goal is for a "good purpose." When we give in to that desire, we place our own will above God's.

The difficulty lies in man's nature. Man-made rules readily become subjective. It's easy to find justification for making rules which are convenient for profit but not for our souls.

I remember a tongue-in-cheek commercial in the 1970s for Hebrew National Hot Dogs. Its tag line was

"We answer to a higher authority." There is both humor and truth in that line. We should follow our Jewish cousins' lead and always "answer to a higher authority."

Once we remember that God is the sacred and that we answer to Him, it changes everything. For the Christian, the demands which God's law puts upon us are the steadfast guide to the prosperity of both work and soul.

How does Christian work differ from that of others? It is *vocation*, work which we consider a calling. We're passionate about it. We are fired up about going to work. We love what we do. Furthermore, our work seeks to *serve others*, not simply to make a profit or to grow the company.

At Anderson Insurance, we have a simple mission: to serve our clients. Our product is insurance, but we never sought to simply "sell a product." Our focus is to provide clients with knowledge and to help them protect their homes and businesses, their finances and their loved ones. To us, selling insurance is a vocation.

The word "vocation" has its roots in the ancient history of the Christian church. It originally refers to God's call for someone to serve in the ministry as priest, pastor, evangelist, deacon, or teacher. An error arose from that history. We began to think that it was only pastors who had vocations. We run from calling. "God hasn't called me. I'm just a businessman."

Yet, the message which we hear from Christian

witnesses at God in the Workplace (GITW) is that *work is* our mission field. We are all pastors, missionaries for Christ in every aspect of our work. Once we recognize that mission, we find *vocation* in whatever work God calls us to do. The employee ceases to be a tool to use and becomes an associate in our task. "The sale" becomes a real client, a person who demands our loyalty, our best work. The boss is no longer a tyrant, but someone whom we respect and for whom we provide our best effort. The competitor is no longer an enemy, but a complement to our common goals of serving our clients.

In comparison to God's work, how does the secular realm define business success? If the sacred does not exist, but secular power and material things are all that matter, then we make our own standards in business. Profit, fame, and especially power become the coin of that realm. There is nothing to check our lust for wealth and for control. Everything becomes a commodity: services, products, sex, babies, children, life, death. We commodify all things from employee production to the price on the stock market to our very lives.

Our lives become a factor of economics to be balanced against an ever growing power structure which seeks to subdue our freedom and our faith. We seek growth at any cost without regard to an ultimate standard. Success in our nation becomes wedded to economic growth. We crunch numbers to decide if we're better off today than last year. We *live* by numbers: by quarterly earnings reports, tax brackets, cost of living adjustments, unemployment numbers, inflation figures, stock reports, interest rates, on and on.

We are impaled by ads which tell us we need *more*! "You *deserve* that bigger house, new car, good skin, healthy glow, newest toy...." We listen and we buy them and work to pay and pay and pay. Don't you feel exhausted? Then let us rest.

Augustine said, "My heart is restless until it rests in thee." We will consider rest in a later chapter, but without God and our knowledge of His sacredness to anchor our work, we inevitably end in loss and desolation. Our work, often stilted, commodified, hopeless and passionless, ends in simple vanity.

"Vanity of vanities, says the Preacher. All is vanity. What does man gain by all the toil at which he toils under the sun?" (Ecc. 1.02) Without God, we gain nothing. There is no goal but empty drudgery and no end but death.

But God sanctifies our work because *He* is sacred. He brings His sacredness into our work. Vocation includes ***productiveness, creativity, fruitfulness and responsibility.***

Jesus tells us ***"My father is working still; and I am working." (John 5.17.)*** The Christian businessman remembers.

"I am the Lord your God…"

Two: Focus on God

"You shall not make for yourself a graven image, or any likeness of anything that is in heaven above, or that is in the earth beneath, or that is the water under the earth; you shall not bow down to them or serve them..."

This is a God who loves us. He did not simply wind up His creation and let it go. He reaches down constantly to find us, to save us, and to bring us home. He cares! He cares about what we do! He cares that we love Him. He made us so that we might know and love Him.

God, our Creator cares so much that He wants our focus to be upon Him. It was that way in the garden before the fall. God always seeks to return us to that state of grace. Even before Jesus came, God reached down with His Commandments to seek our undivided love. ***"You shall not make for yourself a graven image..."***

In the time of Moses, people fashioned gods in various forms and worshiped them. What was their purpose in doing so? They would fashion a god and bow down to it to gain control over a particular problem which plagued them. People worshiped gods to gain favor in war, to fight illness, to ward off death, to stop droughts. (What was it they were doing? In a very real sense, they were practicing the science of that era.)

Invariably, they became enslaved to the perceived demands of the very gods they sought to control. The worst of those gods demanded the sacrifice of infants to satisfy its power. Does that sound familiar?

God brought the Second Commandment to the Israelites because He knew that the worship of other gods or of idols would draw their focus away from His gifts and pollute the purpose to which He had called them.

How does God apply this commandment to us for business? This is the command to focus upon God in work.

Again, He knows us. We are too easily lead away from Him, distracted and tempted to make our own course. We *want* to have our own choices, to make our own way. We want to control *everything* within our lives. *We want it all.*

We do not have to fashion idols by hammering gold and silver onto wood. We only need look around. Business, disconnected from God's restraint, yearns to provide the ready distractions...for a price! American commerce has outperformed any civilization in history in providing such images.

Consider the graven images which draw us away from God today. Screens, big, small and tiny aim distractions in streaming empty images. Temptations at every turn invade our lives from every direction. Sin assaults us at the speed of light. It pulls our attention from our purpose and from God's will and design for us. It transforms us from active, productive people to passive spectators of life.

What is your graven image? To what do we bow down in this age? Celebrity? Political or economic power? Video and computer games? Movies? Money? Facebook? Football? Phone?

The phone, the phone, the phone! Have you glanced at your phone since you started work this morning? How many of us have become enslaved to that one-pound-god in our pockets? How many cannot last an hour without checking it? How many of us carry it into church?

Distractions abound! Our work becomes less productive because we are distracted by the constant stream of emails, texts, tweets, and more. Our isolation grows because we have lost the power to speak to our co-workers and to listen. We no longer look one another in the eye to see the truth of his grace, of her soul.

As owners, do we bow down to the god of profit in business? Are we enslaved to our worthwhile products and efforts to create, to serve and to help through business? If we work to seek control and power beyond God's purpose or if work becomes the center of our lives, even productive work can become an idol. We will soon see how our passion for work can easily slip into obsession.

What is the positive side of this commandment regarding business? We are to focus on God and His will in all that we do. Once we do that, the imperatives and concerns of growing our business, of making expenses or of expanding our market fade away. We are enlivened and enriched. Jesus tells us ***"But seek first his kingdom and his righteousness, and all these things shall be yours as well." (Matt. 6.33)***

My friend, Dave, was the editor of a small town newspaper. I have known few people as happy in their work as he was. His byline had a script over it: *NWNW.* One day, I asked him what it meant. He looked at me for a moment, then said. "No one ever asked me that before. It means, 'Never Worked. Never Will.' I love what I do! This isn't work! It's love."

Here is the essence of vocation. Our work is a calling from God. It derives from the talents He has given us and from the design He has made for our lives. We prevent work from becoming an idol by keeping our **focus on God** and His will for us in every aspect of our lives. That focus includes our business actions.

If God is our focus, it also changes what we produce for the market, how we sell our product, and to whom we bring our services. It is not discrimination if we refuse to support a practice or product which we know promotes sin. It is discernment.

David and Jason Benham have always run their business focused on God's will. In 2014, HGTV had scheduled a TV show featuring their real estate business. However, because they were openly Christian and professed Biblical beliefs about marriage, radical anti-Christian elements started a campaign of lies and pressure. HGTV was forced to cancel the show even before its first episode aired.

They had never discriminated against anyone. The fact that they dared to believe the truth which Christ tells us and were unwilling to compromise their beliefs to go along with the current culture, cost them their show.

They state in their book, Whatever the Cost, "We've always said that we would sell hamburgers, houses, and hula hoops to anyone, but we would not sell to them if it in some way supported or endorsed ideologies that were against our beliefs."[1]

Others may sell what they wish, operate how they choose and care little for their customers. They answer only to this world's legal limits. But we are ***responsible*** in focusing on God. In every aspect, the Christian business will ***focus upon God*** and His will for our business future.

"You shall not make for yourself a graven image."

---

[1] Benham, Whatever the Cost. p. 175

Three: Do First, Say Last

"You shall not take the name of the Lord your God in vain, for the Lord will not hold him guiltless who takes His name in vain."

Our God is a God of the word. ***"And God said, 'Let there be light' and there was light." (Gen.1.3) "In the beginning was the Word, and the Word was God." (John 1.1) "So out of the ground the Lord God formed every beast of the field and every bird of the air, and brought them to the man to see what he would name them...) (Gen. 2.19)***

The spoken word is sacred. It has power. This, too, we have forgotten. We use, abuse, and waste words. God never does. ***"So shall my word be that goes forth from my mouth; it shall not return to me empty, but it shall accomplish that which I purpose, and prosper in the thing for which I sent it. (Isa. 55.11)***

As Christian businessmen, we tread on dangerous ground when we use the name of Jesus, His cross or other Christian symbols to identify our Christian roots. There is danger of taking His name in vain. We must recognize the holiness of the name of God.

What happens when a business takes upon itself

the imprimatur of God and then abuses it? What did Jesus do? Jesus had strong words for the Priests and Pharisees, but there is only one instance in which we find that Jesus seems to lose his temper and become physical.

"The Passover of the Jews was at hand, and Jesus went up to Jerusalem. In the temple he found those who were selling oxen and sheep and pigeons, and the money-changers and overturned their tables. And making a whip of cords, he drove them all, with the sheep and oxen, out of the temple; and he poured out the coins of the money-changers and overturned their tables. And he told those who sold the pigeons, 'Take these things away; it is written My house shall be called a house of prayer, but you have made it a den of thieves.'" (John 2.13-16)

These businessmen were working with the approval of the authorities, providing a needed service for people who came to make offerings to God in the Temple. I am certain the Temple Priests themselves gave their approval. These men were doing business "for God in His house." How could anyone object?

Yet, they drew from Jesus the most violent reaction recorded in the Gospels. Why? Because they had profaned the Temple of God and had used his Name for their own profit. They had imposed upon the hallowed and sacred ground of God's very Temple.

Likewise, as Christian businessmen we must be careful neither to impose upon nor to trade upon the Holy name of Jesus.

The Reverend Terry Fullam, in his study Living the Lord's Prayer, notes that "Hallowed be thy Name" also includes our positive use of God's name. We must take care whenever we use the name of Jesus.

Jesus tells us, ***"Beware of practicing your piety before men in order to be seen by them; for then you will have no reward from your Father who is in heaven." (Matt. 6.1)*** Further, he says, ***"You have heard that it was said to the men of old, 'You shall not swear falsely, but you shall perform to the Lord what you have sworn.' But I say to you, Do not swear at all, either by heaven, for it is the throne of God or by the earth, for it is His footstool…" (Matt. 5.33-34)***

The lesson Jesus references from the Old Testament shows us that we are to "perform to the Lord what you have sworn."

How do we "perform for the Lord?" Jesus has told us to ***"be ye perfect as your father in heaven is perfect." (Matt. 5.48)*** We are held to an almost impossibly high standard when we use His name.

What does that mean for the Christian business? If we place a cross or fish symbol upon our business cards, or state in our mission statement "Our purpose is to honor God in our business," we are calling upon the name of Jesus our Lord. Our performance better match that call.

In the book he wrote with Dr. Steve Steff, The Business Card, Scott Gajewsky shared the story of Peter Freissle, of Polydeck Screen Corporation, who became convicted by the Holy Spirit that he was to run his business on Christian principles.

Under Freissle's leadership, the company radically changed the way they treated their employees, transforming a formerly oppressive work environment into a thriving and caring community. Their product was already the best in the industry, but they committed to make it better and to stand behind its performance no matter what.

It was only after a full transformation of their company that they placed their Core Values based on Christian principles on every business card Peter and his sales force handed out. They found again and again that their bold witness to Christian principles, backed up by the highest standards of performance, brought the company and their employees abundance.

As Christian businesses, we know that the enemy waits to ensnare us, to show our weakness and sin. We must take care as witnesses that our actions rise above any possible taint. Peter tells us ***"Maintain good conduct among the Gentiles, so that in case they speak against you as wrongdoers, they may see your good deeds and glorify God on the day of visitation." (1 Peter 2.12).***

Remember that, in this age, we are among the modern Gentiles, the unbelievers who stand against us and seek to gain advantage from our failings.

Yet, the entire theme of <u>God in the Workplace</u> revolves around the idea that we shall declare boldly that we are Christians doing business, that our work is our mission and that we hold to Christian principals.

How do we balance bold statement and the commandment not to take His name in vain?

We find one answer in the words of Francis of Assisi: "Preach the Gospel at all times; when necessary, use words." Our deeds must speak more boldly than our words. We gain disciples for Christ by winsome deeds, by *being so filled* with the joy of Christ that people see our good deeds and "glorify our Father who is Heaven."

However, in this age when the secular realm condemns, vilifies and silences Christians, we *must* speak boldly. If it is revolutionary to simply speak the name of Jesus in business, then we must stand in revolt. We must do so clearly, with strength, and with winsome love as Pope Francis has recently done.

I have seen, right in GITW, the power of Christ's witness in business. The Spirit moves us as it did Peter at Pentecost. We speak love...and transform lives.

When we do so in business, one knows that we will be challenged. We will be examined and convicted. ***Be ye perfect therefore as your Father in heaven is perfect."*** We are first ***productive,*** before we are verbal.

Use care in declaring the name of Jesus as justification for your business. In all things we are held accountable, not only by those around who watch us and seek to bring charges against our faith, but we also answer to God for the use of His holy name.

"You shall not take the name of the Lord your God in vain."

Four: Rest is Witness

"Remember the Sabbath day, to keep it holy."

God is sacred. Our focus is to be on Him. His name is sacred. His rest is also sacred.

If we are to take actions which preach Jesus within our business, our first action lies within this commandment. ***"Remember the Sabbath..."***

It is not only in this time that commerce is the front line of our battle. It has been so for generations.

It was in the interest of business and commerce that, in the mid Twentieth Century, our nation began to relax the "blue laws" which recognized the Sabbath. We wanted to sell more, produce more, and consume more.

There were industries who stayed open, running twenty-four hours, seven days a week. We wanted to be able to gas our cars, eat at restaurants, or shop at our convenience. After all, back in those days men often worked six days a week for 12 hours a day. We needed the Sabbath to catch up on other things. What was one day? What difference would it make?

What statement did we make as Christians when

we acquiesced and went shopping like everyone else? When our businesses stayed open, we stood against God's law, and gave permission to all society to join us.

What statement do we make *today* as Christian businessmen when we close our businesses on Sunday and invite our employees to enjoy a day of rest? Do you think that Chick-fil-A has had an impact on our culture by their commitment to the Sabbath? Gauge their influence by the size of protest and the vilification which arose from Dan Cathy's simple statement of faith, that he "believed the Bible which says that marriage is between a man and a woman."

Every business which holds and states that belief today is being targeted. But the virulent secular reaction to Chick-Fil-A showed how important their witness in doing business as Christians is for today's world.

Now imagine how much greater an impact we would make if *every* Christian business were to keep the Sabbath? We would revolutionize this nation and transform it overnight. It is just this type of bold statement which is urgently needed. We need to remove the light from under our basket and raise it so that all men might see the saving grace that Christ brings.

My good friend, the Reverend Chris Warner, recently gave a series of sermons on the nature of Christian work. At one point he stressed, "What we do matters and how we work matters. It is how we work in the world that spreads the gospel." He also took a good amount of time to focus on rest. He pointed out that we are tied up in our work because we seek our sense of value through our work rather than by who we are as children of the Lord.

Chris told a story about himself. He also had become caught up in work. "I was getting high on work accolades, raises, successes, etc. I was neglecting my wife and causing fights at home."

Then Chris brought his problem to the Lord. If I might quote him, his prayer was something like, "Dear God, what's *wrong* with my wife? She just won't listen!" And God answered, "*You* are the reason there is a problem. You won't rest because you don't trust me." Chris had made a god out of his work.

Jesus says, ***"Come to me all who labor and are heavy laden, and I will give you rest." (Matt 11.28)*** Rest is as important to the Lord as work. Why? Perhaps because He knows us and knows, more than we admit, that our bodies, minds, and souls need rest.

Rest is an excellent gauge for us to judge if we are working within God's call or have made work an idol. In vocation, God calls us to be passionate about our work. Yet our fallen nature too easily slides from passion to obsession.

How do we tell the difference? We find one way in Luke's account of Martha and Mary. We know the story. Martha had received Jesus into her house. Her sister Mary sat at Jesus' feet and listened to his teaching. Martha was "distracted with much serving" and complained to Jesus to get her sister's help. Jesus' answer is telling: ***"Martha, Martha, you are anxious and troubled about many things; one thing is needful. Mary has chosen the good portion, which shall not be taken away from her.'" (Luke 10.41)***

This statement of Jesus becomes our standard. If our work is making us anxious and troubled, or if it separates us from our loved ones and from God, then we have lost our focus on God.

God's commandment that we rest is already a positive one. It calls for us to rest in Him that we might also celebrate the goodness of His creation and His love for us.

What statement do we make to God when we do not follow the Fourth Commandment? God has said that he would abundantly provide for us. We are to focus on Him and "all these things shall be yours as well." Do we work the Sabbath because we do not trust His word, because we want to make more money, or because we are too driven by our own desire to control our business?

God is steadfast in His promises. If we would simply trust Him and keep His Sabbath, our businesses would thrive and grow. I do not think it an accident that Chick-Fil-A is one of the most successful franchises in America.

One additional step is needed for us to honor the Sabbath. I have a friend who closes his retail store every Sunday. He also refuses to eat out, to shop or to do anything which would require others to serve him.

Imagine if we were to join him in that commitment. Not only would all Christian businesses be closed, but we would honor those workers who are not Christian or not as committed by not requiring that they work. The lack of business would soon encourage non-believers to close, thus providing more workers with rest.

Can we imagine another benefit to the honoring of the Sabbath? Time freed for rest from commerce could bring a new revitalization of the family. If we do not work on Sunday, but gather with family and friends in celebration of our day of rest, we will find family closer and richer than it has been in generations.

Rest prepares us to become more ***fruitful*** in every aspect of our lives, in work and in family.

The first crucial task we are to do if we are to fire a revival of Christ in business is: we are to rest.

"Remember the Sabbath day, to keep it holy."

Five: Perpetuate Witness

"Honor your father and your mother, that your days may be long upon the land which the Lord your God is giving you."

Imagine a God who cares so much for us that He designs an incarnation of His love right within our DNA? ***"...in the image of God he created him; male and female, he created them. And God blessed them, and God said to them, 'Be fruitful and multiply...'" (Gen. 2.27-28)***

God's very first command pertains to parents and children. Do we not expect that our first parents would have taught their children to know and love God? Of course! Do we teach loving God to our children today?

The Fifth Commandment lies at the center of the commandments. The first four define our relationship to God and the last five to other people. Why is this one central?

This commandment looks back to the first four in reverence. In honoring father and mother we mirror and we make real our honor of God. Moreover, the Fifth Commandment looks forward as the foundation for all those which are to follow. It is in honoring father and mother that we build the basis for every relationship with others, that we build all culture, including our business culture.

This commandment includes a promise: ***"that your days may be long upon the land which the Lord your God is giving you."*** How do we interpret that? If I honor my father and mother, am I going to live longer? (My mom would have told you, "Absolutely." I can still hear her gentle voice. "You watch your mouth, young man! I brought you into this world and I can take you back out.") In spite of Mom's promise, this commandment truly relates to *the nation's* perpetuation in the land. More specifically, it relates to the nation of Israel, but it also applies to our nation today.

"...that your days may be long upon the land..." This is speaking about passing on the health of these commandments from one generation to the next. We can only do so if we honor our father and mother. If we listen to their wisdom, learn from their errors and honor the good that they pass on to us, then we will find our way easier and fuller than they did.

In America, we have always believed that each generation would be better off than the last, and that each would gain in wealth and comfort, intelligence and knowledge, morality and justice.

That has been true until our recent past. We no longer believe it. For the first time in our history, a majority of our citizens do not have hope for the future and do not believe their children will be better off.

There is a growing hopelessness in our nation, a sense that we are fading in power and failing in economic and moral terms; that the America we once knew no longer exists--if it ever did.

This has happened in the same period that our children have been taught the following: "Question authority, especially the beliefs and morals of your parents. Who are they to tell you how to live?" This teaching has become rooted within every one of our institutions: education, entertainment, politics, law, and philosophy.

Every part of today's secular culture preaches that man is autonomous, that he makes his own choices, enters freely into the social contract with others, and owes allegiance to no one other than his own conscience apart from any authority. We have rejected our past, and the tradition and history of the church and the nation. We have set out upon a course of our own choosing.

At the same time that we are inundated with the idea of individual autonomy, our sense of futility and hopelessness has swamped our vision of the future. These two trends are connected. When we cease honoring the moral knowledge our father and mother would pass on, we cut away our moral roots. Do we wonder why our society feels rootless and drifting?

I could quote endless social studies which point to the benefits of the nuclear family. Science provides ample evidence that children thrive best when raised in the home of their natural parents, with both parents present and active in their lives.

Yet at every turn, we have sought to destroy or diminish the family. Legal, economic, and political powers all combine to attack the family. In the seemingly final blow against the Christian (and natural) definition of family, our Supreme Court has declared that the family is whatever we *feel* it should be. Marriage is now based on feelings, not on the reality of our past generations or on God's law.

How can one not see the connection between the attack on the family and the increasing lack of caring in our younger generation? This is especially true in those poorer families who are most vulnerable to the economic forces which are set against the nuclear family.

[The family and the honoring of father and mother is a critical point of battle in today's culture. At the end of this book, we will return to the family. How do we protect it, and reach down to lift if back into the position it should hold in our lives? We must return to the family that same sense of passion which drives our dedication to our work. When we connect work to family, church, neighborhood and school, we begin to weave back together something we have lost in this nation: Community. Hold onto this thought until the end of the book.]

Meanwhile we ask how this commandment of honoring father and mother relates to business? In the same way that our parents passed on moral wisdom to us, we are called to pass Christian moral principles in work on to the next generation. This is true whether that next generation consists of children or of our employees.

Christian businesses are called to think both for this day and for the future. Therefore, we must think about perpetuation. When I am ready to retire, do I simply let the business die away? Do I take my golden parachute and fly without concern for those who inherit my efforts?

Obviously, if we have a successful economic business, we want to see it continue to thrive. Have we also taken care that the next generation of leaders carries forward with the same values, and the same Christ-centered vision that we have so carefully tended in our business garden?

Don Wilson spoke at GITW about his friendship and moral partnership in Christ with two business associates: Kip Miller and William Renfrow. They shared their Christian principles with their employees and with each other. These three met often, held each other accountable in their witness, and supported each other. There are several valuable lessons we learn from them.

First, these men in different businesses committed to keep each other focused on God's will. Thus, Proverbs tells us ***"Iron sharpens iron, and one man sharpens another." (Prov. 27.17)***

Second, in standing together, they brought great power to their witness. ***"Though a man might prevail against one who is alone, two will withstand him. A threefold cord is not quickly broken." (Ecc. 4.12)***

Third, they and their wives joined to witness to their children about the future of their businesses. The three families all went on a retreat to discern the future of each company and of the children's role. The parents testified in bold witness to each other's children about the importance of Christ's role in their lives and businesses.

During that retreat, each child himself or herself pledged to continue this vision. These three great witnesses were perpetuating not only the business but also the word and work of Christ within.

These parents raised their young children in homes where Jesus was an integral part of their lives. They planted their families and businesses on the rock of this foundation. They are building still today with abundance and joy.

What did we learn from our parents? What have we taught our children? Have we shared with them the principles we teach at work? Do they realize that we honor God in every aspect of our lives? If we are to be ***fruitful*** as the Lord commanded, we must be so both physically and spiritually.

"Honor your father and your mother that your days may be long in the land."

Six: Speak Life and Love

"You shall not murder."

Here is a God of Life and Love. He seeks to save every one of us. He is steadfast in His love. He goes even to the Cross and stretches out His hands to embrace us and bring us home. He seeks *eternal* life for us. He hates Death. Thus the Commandment, ***"You shall not murder."***

It's easy to see the prohibition of this commandment. ***"You shall not murder."***

Four simple words. Why can we not obey them? We have progressed so far *physically.* However, we are still as savage as Cain. Or if you prefer the secular view, we are still as savage as...savages: cavemen, or brutes.

Animals? We are *more* savage than the animals who kill, because we murder for sport, for spite, or for no reason. If you wish to know the reality of man's progress, look upon our propensity for murder and for war.

What have we in commerce done? We have made a business of murder and of war. We produce the weapons. We commoditize others. We find the means to murder our children in the womb. We create TV shows and video games which fantasize and glorify murder. We profit from the worst of the evil that men do.

But in this work, I am speaking to my brothers and sisters in Christ. Our focus is deeper than the prohibition of physical murder. We have already seen that God cares about those things which we fail to do "in our thoughts, words and deeds." Are there other ways we murder? We return to Jesus in Matthew:

"You have heard that it was said to the men of old, 'You shall not kill; and whoever kills shall be liable to judgment.' But I say to you that every one who is angry with his brother shall be liable to judgment; whoever insults his brother shall be liable to the council, and whoever says, 'You fool!' shall be liable to the hell of fire." (Matt. 5.212-13)

It is easy for most Christians to discern if a particular business promotes murder. But Jesus demands that we move from the deed down into our souls. How many Christians are like me? How many have lost their tempers and cussed out the competitor who just grabbed your largest client, and took twenty percent of your revenue? Have you, in a fit of anger, told an employee what a fool he is?

Have you lost your temper in arguing with your partner over an important purchase which she didn't want you to make? The business needs it! You go to the Lord and ask, "What's wrong with her? Why won't she listen!?" (Sound familiar?)

You wouldn't think about comparing the horror of actual murder to uncontrolled anger which ends in a careless word. Jesus tells us that you would be wrong. He concerns himself again with our *words.* ***"But what comes out of the mouth proceeds from the heart, and this defiles a man. For out of the heart come evil thoughts, murder, adultery, fornication, theft, false witness, slander." (Matt. 15.19)***

Jesus tells us to guard our hearts *and to guard our mouths!* Perhaps Mom was right. "You watch your mouth, young man! I brought you into this world and I can take you out!"

What is the corollary, or the positive side of this? God is Life and Love. If the purpose of the Christian business is two-fold--both to create productiveness and to spread the Gospel--then we are called to speak Life and Love. The word in anger may be a simple lapse, but it becomes habit, and then a way of doing business. We are told by Christ himself that it is the same as murder. When we fail in this, the enemy waits to bring our sin to light, to expose every fault, and to exploit it to bring down the kingdom.

The Christian business speaks Life and Love in every communication whether within to employees or without to others. And the heart of that speaking lies in one word: forgiveness.

How does the God of Love and Life call us to witness in the face of the horror and tragedy of murder? He calls us to Forgiveness, for that is the essence of both Love and Life.

We recently have experienced the power of such forgiveness right in Charleston, SC. Nine Christians of Mother Emmanuel Church were brutally murdered. Thirty-six hours later their family members faced the young man who had murdered their loved ones.

Every one of those Mother Emmanuel Christians told the man that they loved him and forgave him. This was no easy and careless statement of philosophy. This was the gut wrenching, soul shaking stand of broken people who would not seek vengeance, but who brought forgiveness. I do not know if I would have had the strength of their faith. They are heroes in my eyes.

A pebble thrown into the still pond sends ripples out upon its waters. The ripples of their courage still resonate out into our nation. They witness to the Life and Love of God.

Now this same God--who hates murder--calls us to visit murderers in prison and to bring his good news. One witness in GITW, Greg McCool spoke about a ministry which lies at the junction of work and murder.

Jump Start Vision is a Faith Based Prison Rehabilitation program in Spartanburg. It brings Christ into prison for those who are going to be released. This program is designed to teach those men authority, accountability, and responsibility. Among the prisoners are some who have served time for murder. We remember the Psalm, ***"The Lord sets the prisoners free." (Ps. 146.7)***

These men had been justly imprisoned for deeds they had done. They were prisoners also of their own guilt and self-hatred. The vision of this ministry lifts them up, fills them with the certainty of God's Love and Life, and provides the means to teach and track their progress.

A strong part of this program is providing work for these men when they are released from prison. The organizers seek businesses who will become partners in reaching out to these men to provide productive work. The program has had incredible success in reducing the recidivism rate from an average of 67 percent to less than 3 percent.

Here is a program which takes the convicted sinner, seeks to redeem him from sin, seeks his repentance and reformation, and guides him to return to the fold of God's love. This is Jesus Christ in action.

The Christian response to the Sixth Commandment is twofold. We guard our mouths with Life and Love and our hearts with Forgiveness. We ***create*** the means for Christ to work within our hearts and our businesses to expand his Kingdom. It is never easy, but we have been called.

"You shall not murder."

Seven: Integrity is Steadfast Love

"You shall not commit adultery."

God is a God of steadfast love. His passion for us never fades. This is not passion as in some uncontrolled emotion or a feeling which flames bright and then burns out. This is the Passion of a God who takes on our form, who in lowliness walks to the Cross to take upon Himself all our sin, and who will *not* give sin and death its due. This is a God for whom steadfast love is the *only* love.

He calls us into a relationship which mirrors that passionate and steadfast love: marriage. ***"This at last is bone of my bones and flesh of my flesh; ...Therefore a man leaves his father and his mother and cleaves to his wife, and they become one flesh." (Gen. 2.23-24)*** Thus was marriage designed by God.

Imagine how Adam must have said those words. Remember the passion which you had for your bride on the day you faced her at the altar of God to pledge your eternal love. This is the incarnation of God's love in man. This is the holiest edifice on God's earth, the place where man's love and God's entwine.

But in America, we have burned that holy place almost to the ground. We have breached the defensive walls and invited the enemy in to feed our willful lusts. The enemy takes no prisoners. He kills and destroys. He tramples all into the dirt of sin and death. We care not for our wives or husbands, nor for our children.

"You shall not commit adultery." When asked by the Pharisees why Moses allowed divorce under the law, Jesus answered, ***"For your hardness of heart, Moses allowed you to divorce your wives, but from the beginning it was not so." (Matt 20.8)*** Our hardness of heart in America must exceed that of the Israelites' by a geometric and immeasurable portion.

Has adultery had an impact upon business? No answer is necessary. Temptation abounds in our workplaces, and we are infamously bad at resisting it. ***"And if you do not do well, sin is couching at the door; its desire is for you, but you must master it." (Gen. 4.7)***

Let's be very clear. It is not the fault of women in the workplace. We are all subject to temptation.

Our best response to temptation in our business is to follow the example of Billy Graham. He refused to ever be alone with a woman other than his wife. Here is a giant of modern Christianity, who was dedicated passionately to his wife, Ruth. We would think if anyone could resist, he could. But Graham knew himself better than most of us do. Temptation is too close and too strong for most of us, even the saints among us.

What then is the standard we are to follow? Jesus again presents us the most difficult one. ***"I say to you that every one who looks at a woman lustfully has already committed adultery with her in his heart." (Matt. 5.28)***. Jesus calls us to model the steadfast love which the Father has for us. He reminds us of the passion which we feel for our wives or husbands. He calls us to integrity.

Even secular law recognizes the reality of integrity. It has established laws to try to prevent sexual combat in the workplace. Sexual harassment is illegal. Affairs are okay as long as both parties consent. That is, until one is fired. Then he or she *will* sue. Employment Practices is a thriving part of the law. Most of that law refers to the issues and temptations of sexual interplay among workers.

What is the positive aspect for this commandment? To find it, we return to the opening ideas of the steadfast love of God and His passion for us. In mirroring this foundation of God's Passion, we begin to build an edifice within our workplace which reflects God's integrity. It is built upon the recognition of the inherent dignity and integrity of every person working for us.

Be warned. We cannot build this in our workplace without first grounding our marriages in Christ's love. The first step of infidelity is the loss of that passion which is the reflection of His love for us. It is only in refreshing, each day, that passionate love for spouse that we will maintain our faithfulness. When we do, the power of that faithfulness and integrity will shine in every manner and deed.

In this day of easy divorce and in the atmosphere of open and uncommitted sex, this is extremely difficult. Yet we must not give in to this age. We are to witness through our work to the power of Christ's love within our lives.

Marital fidelity is only one aspect of integrity which we consider in business, but every other aspect mirrors it. What we will discover is that integrity is the single most powerful gift which our business will ever possess.

The power of integrity is what carried the Benham Brothers through their trials and defended them against false accusations. Integrity is the sure witness of those bold Christians who have stood upon their certain knowledge of God's law when that stance could possibly cause them to lose everything.

Integrity must run throughout the organization. It cannot be compartmentalized. We cannot maintain witness as Christian businessmen while being unfaithful in our marriages. Do we find it easier to lie to our wives when we have lied to gain the business? We cannot hope to have integrity in our company when we direct someone to steal corporate secrets.

Every form of sin is an attempt to shortcut the work needed to gain a God-given value. Adultery is the shortcut which desires to use another's body to satisfy a lust in our own. It does not honor or commit to that other person. It denies his or her value. It denies our own, while using simple material physical sensations as a substitute for the deepest joy we might experience.

If we are to follow God's laws within business, our watchword in every part of our edifice must be integrity, which is personal ***responsibility*** both within our hearts and without. It is the only way in which we will be able to witness.

"***You shall not commit adultery.***"

Eight: Create Abundance

"You shall not steal."

We return to God, the productive worker. ***"My Father is working still, and I am working." (John 5.17)*** "***And God said, 'Let there be a firmament in the midst of the waters..." (Gen. 1.6) "And God saw everything that He had made, and behold, it was very good." (Gen. 1.31)***

Look around you at the sheer beauty and abundance of the natural world in God's creation. There are millions of creatures, awe inspiring, whimsical, varied beyond any imagination we might have. God fills creation with joy. The creation *is* His joy. Work is His joy. He delights in our work also.

Think back upon the time when God gave these commandments. Imagine yourself a young Israelite. Moses is reading from the tablets of the law. You know this God who has brought you out of the land of Egypt. You remember your life and the generations of your elders going back 400 years. For all that time you and your forebears worked and toiled, never knowing the joy of receiving the products of your effort. There was no certainty of reward, but only of endless work and punishment, until death. Work. Only work. Your hands and back are broken with it. Then, someone comes, takes the product of your effort and steals it away.

Now you hear the word of God. "You shall not steal." Tears come to your eyes and those around you begin to weep, for God has brought back to you the blessing of work, that you will enjoy the abundance of its fruits. Your work is blessed by this Holy God, and protected by the imprimatur of His law against those who would steal it from you.

Several of the witnesses at GITW have noted that God created work for man before the fall. Work was "good." As Chris Warner notes, it only became filled with thistles and thorns *after* the fall.

For so many people in America today, it seems that work is drudgery. We awaken on Monday dreaming about Friday and TGIF. We complain so readily. We have no idea of the hardships our brothers in the third world face. They awaken on Monday--and every day--not knowing where they will find the next meal; not knowing if this day will simply continue in hunger or end in oppression and death.

When we go on mission trips to those places, we are inspired by the peace and faith of those who possess so little. We are humbled by the power which they have for happiness, a power based in Christ Jesus.

The Christian church and Christian businesses have given more to bring these places out of poverty than any other entity in history. Yet there is always more that we must do. We are called to share from our abundance and we will do so.

What is the deeper place which calls to us from within this commandment? Contemplate the difference between the two worlds mentioned above and our attitudes about our work. Those who know real absolute poverty and grinding work seem to have a much richer joy in the Lord.

What have we lost in gaining wealth and comfort? We have become inured to the blessings of God *because* they are so abundant!

As owners, it is easy to take our employees for granted and see them only as human tools. In The Business Card, Scott Gajewsky speaks of the way the employees were treated before Peter Freissle was convicted by the Holy Spirit. They were pushed until close to breaking. The work atmosphere was toxic and confrontational.

When Freissle made Christ the center of his business, the transformation was radical. The employees became partners in work. Their jobs became more fulfilling, their co-workers real people. They began to lift one another and to help. They became a community. Unsurprisingly, their production and the quality of their work improved dramatically.

The Christian business seeks a stronger relationship between employee and employer. It is deeper than simply a fair wage paid for fair work. If our employee is more than simply a human tool, his value and his life become of utmost concern.

Paul's letter to Philemon is the only personal letter included in the Bible. Paul is writing to Philemon regarding Onesimus, a runaway slave who had become a Christian under Paul's tutelage. On realizing that Onesimus is Philemon's slave, Paul immediately directs his return.

But now, Onesimus is no longer a human tool. As a Christian, his status is suddenly and completely different. Paul asks Philemon to receive Onesimus not as the slave who stole from him and ran away, but as a brother in Christ, ***"...that you might have him back for ever, no longer as a slave, but more than a slave--a well beloved brother, most of all to me, and how much more to you, both as a man and a Christian. If you consider me your partner, receive him as you would receive me." (Philemon 15-17)***

This is how all Christian business owners should look upon employees: as brothers in Christ, and of inestimable value.

As Christian employees, how do we respond to the abundance of God's gifts through our jobs? Too often, we take the comfort and ease of the job for granted and become apathetic to God's call for our role in business. God wants our work to be productive. When we fail in our effort by shirking the duties we had taken on, from whom do we steal? From ourselves? Perhaps. From the boss? Probably. From God? Certainly. He has given us great talents and we fail so often to even begin to use them properly. (Confession: guilty!)

In Paul's letter to Philemon, we again see the reference to how we should act. ***"Formerly he was useless to you, but now he is indeed useful to you and to me." (Philemon 11)*** When we are infused with Christ, our work becomes vocation. We seek to do our best for ourselves, our employer and for God.

Our God is a God of abundance. In the Christian business, an abundance of good will and of investing in one another reigns in the relationship of employer and employee.

God entrusts us with the talents he has given us. Do we remember the parable which Jesus told of the talents? It is a different kind of talent, a form of money. The parable gives us pause to reflect.

"For it will be as when a man going on a journey called his servants and entrusted to them his property; to one he gave five talents, to another two, to another one, to each according to his ability. ...After a long time, the man returned. ...He also who had received the one talent came forward, saying 'Master, I knew you to be a hard man, reaping where you did not sow, and gathering where you did not winnow; so I was afraid, and I went and hid your talent in the ground. Here you have what is yours.' But his master answered him, 'You wicked and slothful servant! You knew that I reap where I have not sowed, and gather where I have not winnowed? Then you ought to have invested my money with the bankers, and at my coming I should have received what was my own with interest....And he cast the worthless servant into the outer darkness; there men will weep and gnash their teeth.'" (Matt. 25. 14-30)

When the Master returned, "after a long time," it was to reclaim his *own* property. None of the talents was owned by the servants. The wise servants used the talents given them to expand the master's wealth. God seeks for us to use the talents He has given to expand the wealth which is His Kingdom.

Jesus told many parables about the owner of the vineyard and the tenants, or about a King and his servant, or the bridegroom and the maidservants. These were the employees of that time.

These parables are meant to point us to our relationship to Jesus himself and to our readiness to welcome the Owner, the Bridegroom, or the King when He returns. But we can also learn from them what the right relationship is between owner and employee.

For Christians, *none* of us is the true owner of his business. We are *all* employees entrusted with different talents. We are all called to an accounting when "after a long time," the true Owner returns. We are entrusted to be ***productive*** for his Kingdom, as employer or employee.

When we fulfill that trust, God's reward is great. "For to every one who has will more be given, and he will have abundance..." (Matt. 25.29)

"You shall not steal."

Nine: Complementition

"You shall not bear false witness against your neighbor."

We return to the word. Words are crucial. God spoke Creation into existence. Jesus is the Word. Adam named all the birds and beasts. Jesus warned us often to guard our words as much as our hearts.

Words...create. Do you realize that scientists are still living the call of Genesis? What is the first thing they do when they discover a new species or element? They *name* it.

When the businessman brings a new product or process to fruition, he agonizes over the *name*. "What do I call it? It has to have a catchy name! A name that will give it life! A name that will make people want to see it, touch it and own it."

Words have real power. They make into reality what once was only idea. They also have the power to make falsehood real in the sense that it can come to life.

Do we remember the commandment that we are not to take the Lord's name in vain? The name of the Lord was so holy that the Hebrews would not even say it. In ancient times, people believed that names had power. Perhaps they saw a reality which we fail to understand in our modern era.

Words were especially crucial in any legal dispute. Until very recently, there was no system of "evidence" in judging a crime. If a person were accused of a crime, two or three witnesses were gathered to testify against him before a judge. That testimony could determine a loss of property or even death for the defendant.

Sometimes the plaintiff would hire witnesses to "testify" against his opponent. Without objective proof, there was no appeal which would save the man against whom they testified. The practice had become rampant in the ages before Moses.

For God, the word is sacred. His Word became incarnate, and became man. How will God look upon the man who would lie under oath? His commandment tells us. "You shall not bear false witness."

Our Christian understanding of "bearing false witness" goes much deeper. As I said before, words create. If we consider the Sixth Commandment and how we found that words could be as sinful as murder, we begin to see the application of this commandment.

To utter a curse in anger against an opponent is evil enough. Bearing false witness rises beyond the curse. It takes the word and makes it action by speaking the lie to another person. The lie takes on its own life and begins to gain reality.

In the world of business, this is especially

damaging. Our greatest asset is our reputation. It takes years of effort and care to build and to nurture the soil in which it grows. Yet in one night our enemy can come and sow the weeds of false witness. People begin to whisper. Doubt takes hold, and then becomes conviction.

"It couldn't be true!"

"Well, there must be something to it! Otherwise, why would we have heard it?"

"I guess you're right."

What is the positive goal we Christians seek in business? Healthy competition, yes! I want to win that new account even more than my rival. Christians don't need to shy away from competition.

But I refuse to win the account by speaking against that competitor, even if the words I use are true. There are dishonest people in every business. Some people will shade the truth, bend the rules beyond breaking, even lie. I cannot stand that they do so. Yet I will not bring any kind of witness against them to a third party in order to increase my business.

I have always practiced what I call "complementition" rather than competition. No business can be all things to all buyers (though certain on-line companies are working hard to be).

When I began in the insurance business, one of the first things I realized was that a certain well known company could write home and auto policies in one area much more competitively than I could. I began recommending them.

The owner of that agency called me after a few weeks. "What are you doing? Why are you recommending us?"

"Because, your product in this area is better than mine."

"But you're my competition!"

"Yes, but I tell the prospect the truth up front, and help them by sending them to you. I'd rather do that than sell them much more expensive insurance for the same coverage...and have them find out later that they could have bought it cheaper. They appreciate it."

He laughed. "So do I. Thanks. I'll make sure to send things we can't handle your way."

He's been a good friend for over 25 years. We complement each other's business and trust that we can send people to one another. By the way, I have gained a lot more in writing large accounts he sent me than I would have trying to compete where business didn't fit.

Does the positive word bear fruit? We find the answer again in Philemon. Paul writes to his friend,

"It is with complete confidence in your willingness to listen that I write to you, for I know well that you will do more than I ask." (Philemon 21)

In his study of Philemon, William Barclay notes that, "it is typical of Paul's dealings with people. It was his rule always to expect the best from others; he never really doubted that Philemon would grant his request. It is a good rule. To expect the best from others is often to be more than half-way to getting it..."[2]

It *is* a good rule to expect the highest of others. It is our duty as Christians to do so. We may often be disappointed by others. However, many people will see our belief in them and then do respond.

As Christians, we ***create*** good with our words. In bearing false witness, others create enmity, division and strife.

The Christian businessman finds that the positive word ***creates*** abundance. When we speak well of our rivals, the client's trust in us goes up. The industry we work in is made better for it. Good words create. False ones destroy.

"You shall not bear false witness..."

---

2 William Barclay; The Letters to Timothy, Titus, and Philemon; c,1975 Westminster John Knox Press

Ten: Give

"You shall not covet your neighbor's house; you shall not covet your neighbor's wife, nor his male servant, nor his female servant, nor his ox, nor his donkey, nor anything that is your neighbor's."

After all the previous commandments, after the requirements to keep God sacred in our lives, to honor father and mother, to speak and do His will, after murder and theft and adultery and lying, then coveting seems just so...small.

Until we realize that coveting was the very first sin.

"So when the woman saw that the tree was good for food, and that it was a delight to the eyes, and that the tree was to be desired to make one wise, she took of its fruit and ate;" (Gen. 3.6)

This one sin split apart our relationship with God, and brought into the world enmity between creatures, pain in childbirth, sin, and death. Adam and Eve coveted.

All the other commandments address deed and word. This last one now addresses our hearts. Coveting is not an action, but a state of mind and soul. To covet encompasses a desire for the unearned. It raises the ego above reality, seeking to bend what *is* into what we *want.* It is the desire to *be God,* no matter what it is that we covet.

Coveting taps into the ultimate idol: me, because I have put my desires above God's will and law.

It embraces envy which desires the destruction of the neighbor against whom we covet. Thus, we murder him in our hearts.

It lusts after that which the neighbor owns or has. The one who covets commits adultery in his heart.

It steals the goodwill of the neighbor.

It bears false witness against him, seeking to claim, for oneself, what he owns.

Coveting is the source of all sin. It is the dark heart out of which pours all the evil of which Jesus speaks. "***For out of the heart come evil thoughts, murder, adultery, fornication, theft, false witness, slander. These are what defile a man." (Matt. 15.19-20)***

What is the positive force which we use to combat this horror? It is Giving. God calls us to give freely. He asks for only a tithe, but that is to be the "first fruits" of the harvest. What that meant was we are to give the finest ten percent: We pledge not the leftovers, not the rump roast, but the filet mignon.

Mark tells us, ***"Jesus sat down opposite the treasury, and watched the multitude putting money into the treasury. Many rich people put in large sums. And a poor widow came, and put in two copper coins, which make a penny.***

And he called his disciples to him, and said to them, "Truly, I say to you, this poor widow has put in more than all those who are contributing to the treasury. For they all contributed out of their abundance, but she out of her poverty has put in everything she had, her whole living." (Mark 12.41-44)

We have such abundance from which to give. We must make certain that our giving reflects the deep gratitude we have for the blessings God has given us.

In giving, we fulfill all of the Genesis characteristics of work. We share our ***productivity*** and ***fruitfulness*** in the most ***creative*** and ***responsible*** way possible.

God calls us to give joyfully and generously.

He calls us to reach out to the "least of these;" to care for widows and orphans.

He calls us to give of the talents he gifted to us.

He calls us to know that all which we own is simply His gift to us. We are the tenants in the vineyard. We are the watchmen at the tower, or the bridesmaids awaiting the groom. We are His witnesses.

He calls us to thankfulness for His love and for His son, Jesus Christ.

He calls business to share in the abundance of His love, and thereby to transform the marketplace into a holy place.

In summary, is there a proper place for worship, for witness, and for mission? Are we right to bring Jesus Christ into our business to make it holy? Jesus answers us as he does the Samaritan woman at the well.

"Woman, believe me, the hour is coming when neither on this mountain nor in Jerusalem will you worship the Father....the hour is coming, and now is, when the true worshipers will worship the Father in spirit and truth..." (John 4.21,23)

My wife and I went on a trip to the Holy Land. When I stood at the Western Wall of the Temple and touched it, I felt an absolute certainty. The Lord was not there. In today's world, He is not in a Temple in Jerusalem. Nor is he on a mountain in Samaria as the woman at the well thought he might be. Jesus has come down. He has brought His Holy Spirit to dwell within us. He is here now. Here within your heart. Here.

"Do you not know that you are God's temple and that God's Spirit dwells in you?" (1 Cor. 3.16)

Jesus Christ has called us to witness, in life and in business. The only commandment Jesus gave to us is quite simple:

"Go therefore and make disciples of all nations." (Matt. 28.19)

The Next Steps

"The harvest is plentiful, but the laborers are few; pray therefore the Lord of the harvest to send out laborers into his harvest." (Matt. 9.37)

"Do you not say, 'There are four months, then comes the harvest?' I tell you, lift up your eyes, and see how the fields are already white for harvest." (John 4.35)

We are extremely fortunate in Charleston. We live in a place called "The Holy City." There is good reason for that name. In this city, the abundance of the Holy Spirit and the Gospel of Jesus Christ are overflowing.

God has been moving among the people of South Carolina, especially within the marketplace community. Shortly after I presented The Ten Commandments for Business, we were blessed when The South Carolina Christian Chamber of Commerce planted a chapter here in Charleston.

This Christian Chamber has been in preparation to launch a new and higher vision in 2017. We seek to impact South Carolina for Christ through engaging commerce, culture and community. This vibrant movement is just beginning to take form and is creating excitement in businesses, churches and giving organizations all over the state. I am privileged to serve as the Charleston area director for the SC Christian Chamber and look forward to helping provide a unified voice for Christ in the marketplace.

The SC Christian Chamber is an ecumenical movement. We believe that we represent the body of believers. As our vision states, "We see the Body of Christ as the entire Christian community and envision commerce and commUNITY working together through a Biblical Worldview to bring unity among Christians in South Carolina."

Our Charleston community mirrors this vision. We are an ecumenical area. We have strong Catholic, Anglican, Baptist and Evangelical school systems. We have one of the premier private Christian Universities in the South, Charleston Southern University.

CSU reaches out to business to mentor Christ's way, and business responds. 2016 marked the fifteenth Charleston Leadership Foundation Prayer breakfast where over a thousand of the faithful gathered to hear a Ed Kobel witness to his Christian walk in business. Hundreds gather quarterly at Lifeworks for fellowship based in Christian principles. The other eight months have God in the Workplace, whose growing ministry reaches people thirsty for the movement of God in the marketplace.

Churches of every denomination, from Orthodox to Evangelical, thrive and share, work and pray together.

I believe we are seeing the first rays of light of that morning sunrise which will see the union of God's church into the One Church, His body. We are witnessing that beginning here today in Charleston. That movement may take a hundred or a thousand years, but we have seen its birth here!

We build up one another in the faith. We celebrate victories and mourn loss together. We bridge differences in His name. This is the reality of who we are in this Holy City. This is the reality hidden within our state: an underlying swift current of life-giving water, which is the Christian Church. William Renfrow, the visionary leader of the SC Christian Chamber often says, "We are the most Christian state in the nation. It's time to stand up and let people know that we are!"

As Jesus commissioned his disciples to ***"Go therefore and make disciples of all nations,"*** so we are called to refresh that good news in America.

That revival for America begins here in South Carolina. The battle is joined already. Our brothers in commerce were the first to surrender, and to retreat in the battlefields of the last century. We in business will be the front line in this new century, and become the point of the spear in this new battle.

Our mission is to plant new marketplace ministries. We begin by building the body of Christ through the mission and vision of the SC Christian Chamber. We will then begin to take that vision out to every part of our nation.

In September of 2015, Sam Lam of the Manas Development Group described the planting of Mission Churches among businesses in foreign lands like Dubai and Malaysia. In the same way, we need to plant our missions of Christian Chambers of Commerce in every state.

The Christian Chamber will reach out vertically within our own community, bringing together the resources which our communities need to once again thrive. We must bring ministry into schools to return God to education. We begin by mentoring students just as business reaches out to high school and college students by seeking interns. We need God in the Schools.

From the schools, we reach out into the street to find the dealers and the gangs, in order to teach them that God values them, and to teach them skills to find productive work. We must build roadblocks to stop their inevitable march towards prison.

From the streets we reach back into the family, in the homes where aunts and mothers and grandmothers despair at the loss of their children's innocence. We reach out to the young teen mother who is in desolation, desperate for someone simply to be there. We mentor Christian commitment to bring to young fathers a place and purpose for their desire for true manhood.

God in the Workplace, God in the School, God in the Street, God in the Family. Finally we bring in the harvest to the Owner of the Vineyard. We return the lost sheep back into the fold of the church.

When the families of the Mother Emmanuel Saints reached out in love to forgive the one who murdered their loved ones, they began a transformation of this nation. We are called to echo and to further that change. The transformation will not come from Washington, D.C. or Columbia downward. It is not political. It is not of Caesar, but of Christ.

This revolution in America comes from the deepest levels of our nation: from the family facing loss with grace; from the individual whose heart is broken by the sure knowledge of his own sin; from the business person seeking the deeper roots of God's call.

We are a nation thirsting for the truth, starving for purpose and meaning within our lives. We know that there is a deep hole within us which yearns for something, but we have forgotten the cornerstone of our nation's laws and of our own hearts.

"I will put my law within them, and I will write it upon their hearts; and I will be their God and they shall be my people." (Jer. 32.33)

The presence of God made the whole mountain of Sinai quake. The same quake tore apart the veil of the temple on that dark afternoon in Jerusalem. The veil, which separated the Father from us, was torn in two--not by the power of anger but by the power of love.

The same quake has started a wave, rising from the depths of an ocean which is the love of Jesus Christ.

Do you feel its pulse in your heart? It is a tidal wave rising to encompass Charleston and to surge onward. It will flood this nation in a revival of the Holy Spirit. Do you feel it? Look to the East. It is coming with the rising Son.

Come, Lord Jesus. America awaits.

"The light shines in the darkness, and the darkness has not overcome it." (John 1.5)

The Ten Commandments For Business

I. I am the Lord your God.
You shall have no other gods before me.
The Sacred exists.

II. You shall not make any graven image.
Focus on God.

III. You shall not take the name of the Lord in vain
Do First, Speak Last

IV. Remember the Sabbath day to keep it Holy.
Rest is Witness.

V. Honor your father and your mother.
Perpetuate Witness.

VI. You shall not murder.
Speak Life and Love.

VII. You shall not commit adultery.
Integrity is Steadfast Love.

VIII. You shall not steal.
Create Abundance.

IX. You shall not bear false witness.
Complementition.

X. You shall not covet.
Give.

A NOTE FROM THE AUTHOR:

Some will criticize this book for being too general. For example, there are obviously many businesses who are not operating with Christian principles, but who treat employees well, make excellent products, and operate morally.

Whether or not they realize it, those businesses are operating on the same Ten Commandments principles I have outlined here. As I said, "The Ten Commandments are not only right, they are practical."

Despite what this culture may teach, there are objective moral laws which apply to every situation, in every culture throughout history. Every civilization has expressed principles whose purest form is in the Ten Commandments. Those principles apply equally to individual lives and to business applications.

I have often heard a similar argument. "One of the most moral men I know is an atheist. In fact, he's much more honest than many Christians I know."

My answer to that statement is the same as my answer here. To the extent which he is acting with moral principle, he is acting under universal moral law. If he could look deeply within himself using an objective eye, he would find that he is following The Ten Commandments. He would find that there is no other way to live on this earth.

I can attest to the truth of that assertion, for I was once that man: an atheist lost to God. The story of how I fled from God's calling, just as America is fleeing, will be published in "Call Me Jonah."

ABOUT THE AUTHOR

Besides his Christian commentary in The Ten Commandments For Business, Joseph P. Stringer has written novels, a children's illustrated book, music, poetry and other social commentary. His works have been published in various venues in the Charleston, South Carolina area and are also available on Amazon.

The U-Pick Farm was published in early 2014 and is a delight for children from ages 2 to 12. Read it to them and they'll insist that you take them picking.

The novels are set in America in the near future. Stringer is not sure if these books, first envisioned in the 1980s, are fantasy or prophesy. In The Gem Testament, Christians have been pushed out of any public setting--something which is coming true today. The Chosen finds them hunted throughout America.

Watch for upcoming releases in 2017:

The Ten Commandments for Life: A reflection on how the Ten Commandments direct us to lives which are filled with grace and love.

Call Me Jonah: Like Jonah, Joseph Stringer ran from God's calling. America, too, has run far from God's clear call for her to be a witness of Christ's saving grace for the world.

The Passion of God: We are designed by God to be passionate about work, worship and witness.

Contact the author at:
www.tencommandmentsforbusiness.com

May God, the Father, Son and Holy Spirit, bless us.

www.ingramcontent.com/pod-product-compliance
Lightning Source LLC
Chambersburg PA
CBHW032213040426
42449CB00005B/576